The Great Market

The Great Market: *a survey of nine hundred years of Norwich provision Market*

Ursula Priestley

Centre of East Anglian Studies
University of East Anglia

Contents

FRONT COVER
    The Market from Jarrold's corner
BACK COVER
    Norwich Market Place
    Thomas Rowlandson, 1788
    (Norfolk Museums Service)

ISBN 0 906219 25 6
© Centre of East Anglian Studies 1987
Centre of East Anglian Studies
University of East Anglia
Norwich NR4 7TJ

Designed by Richard Malt

Front cover photograph by Tom Mackie, Norwich
Photoset in Baskerville by Spire Origination Ltd, Norwich
Printed by Witley Press, Hunstanton, Norfolk

Preface & acknowledgements

THROUGHOUT the nine hundred years of its recorded history Norwich has been a leading regional capital, a premier market town, and a centre of trade and commerce. Geographically, the city was a natural distribution point for the agricultural produce of much of East Anglia and it was also the major outlet for a large community of urban craftsmen, as well as the mart for many merchants from this country and overseas. The huge provision Market, on which most of this trade was focused, was famous for its size and for the diversity of merchandise on sale, making it a tourist attraction long before the twentieth century. The eighteenth-century historian, Francis Blomefield, described it as 'the grandest market in all England'.

Within the limited scope of this booklet, it would have been impossible to attempt a comprehensive history over such a long time-span. Instead, the city's rich collection of manuscript and published material has been used to present a series of studies chosen to illustrate the multi-faceted life of the Market at various periods in its long past.

If an impression is left of uninterrupted prosperity and success, this is probably because the bad times tend to be less well documented than the good. It would be a false picture. Norwich, like all cities, suffered periods of difficulty, unrest, and decline, and the Market's fortunes fluctuated in line with those of the city and its region. After the Black Death in 1349, many of the stallholders died or fled to the country and stalls were left in ruins; while in a time of severe depression in the mid-sixteenth century it is recorded that the market-place was overgrown with weeds. So the endurance of this Norwich institution over so many centuries is remarkable – the more so since its extent remains undiminished and, indeed, has been enhanced by twentieth-century improvements.

Among many people to whom I am indebted, first thanks must go to Margot Tillyard, who has generously made available the results of her recent work on the city's medieval deeds to compile the map on page 8. I am also grateful to the Clerk of the Markets and his deputy; the Norfolk Museums Service; the Norfolk Records Office; and not least to the staff of the Local Studies Library, whose deep knowledge of their nineteenth-century collections has enabled them to unearth for me some of the fascinating prints and photographs used as illustrations. Dr P.J. Corfield, Elizabeth Stern, Dr Tom Williamson, Dr Richard Wilson, and Rachel Young have been kind enough to read and comment on the text. Maps have been drawn by Philip Judge, Martin Leverington, and David Luckhurst.

The Helen Sutermeister Memorial Fund has made a generous donation towards the costs of publication.

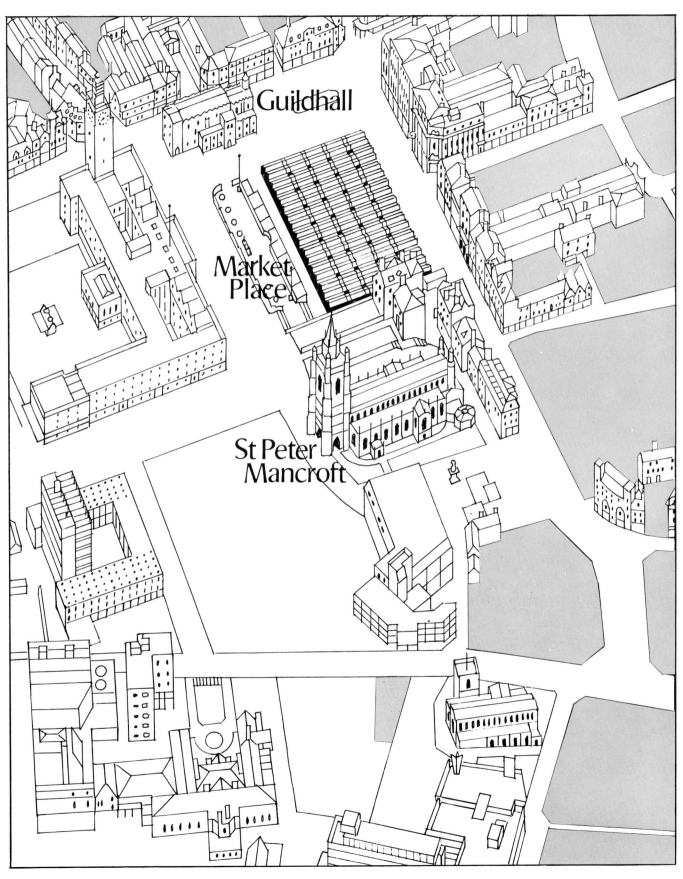

Guildhall

Market
Place

St Peter
Mancroft

Origins

THE Norwich provision Market, like the Castle and the Cathedral, is a legacy of the Norman Conquest. At the time of the invasion, Norwich was already an established, organized, and flourishing community, handling the trade of a wide and prosperous hinterland. It was one of the largest and most important boroughs in the kingdom – a rich prize for the conquerors. The market and administrative centre of the pre-Norman town was Tombland, situated at the convergence of the main roads coming in from the country. With the building of the Castle and Cathedral after the Conquest, an area of French influence straddled the town, superimposing new building on the old street pattern – a circumstance from which traffic flow in the city has never altogether recovered.

At Norwich, as elsewhere, the Normans created a new borough of their own alongside the old one. This lay immediately west of the Castle and its defensive earthworks in a district known as 'Mancroft'; and the new town was eventually called 'Newport'. The Market was part of it, immediately established to supply and accommodate the Norman burgesses and merchants who built houses near the Castle, and perhaps to provision the large garrison stationed there. The 1086 Domesday lists a market in Mancroft, and it seems likely that, by degrees, this supplanted the old market in Tombland to become the primary focus of the city's commercial life. The building of a Tollhouse – almost certainly on the site of the present Guildhall – would have followed closely on the establishment of the new Market, in order to provide a collecting point for the tolls and taxes exacted by the Crown. Before long, although exactly when it is impossible to say, the Tollhouse assumed the additional functions of civil and judicial headquarters.

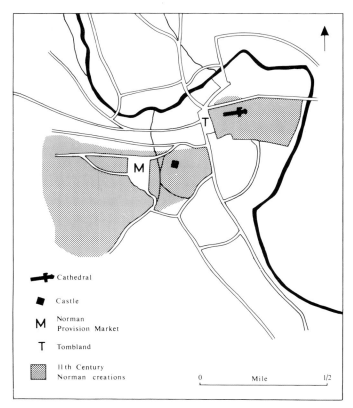

✠	Cathedral
■	Castle
M	Norman Provision Market
T	Tombland
▦	11th Century Norman creations

0   Mile   1/2

The Norman town

Apart from the existence of a Tollhouse, we know almost nothing about the processes of trade in this early market. Not until the city archives become more comprehensive towards the end of the thirteenth century can we work out the identity of stallholders, the range of their merchandise, and the local regulations governing their trade.

An aerial impression of the present-day market area. Redrawn by David Luckhurst from his 'Norwich: an architectural map'
(published by the Centre of East Anglian Studies)

Tombland, the market-place and administrative centre of the pre-Norman town. This drawing, looking south, by David Hodgson, is dated 1827.
(Norfolk Museums Service)

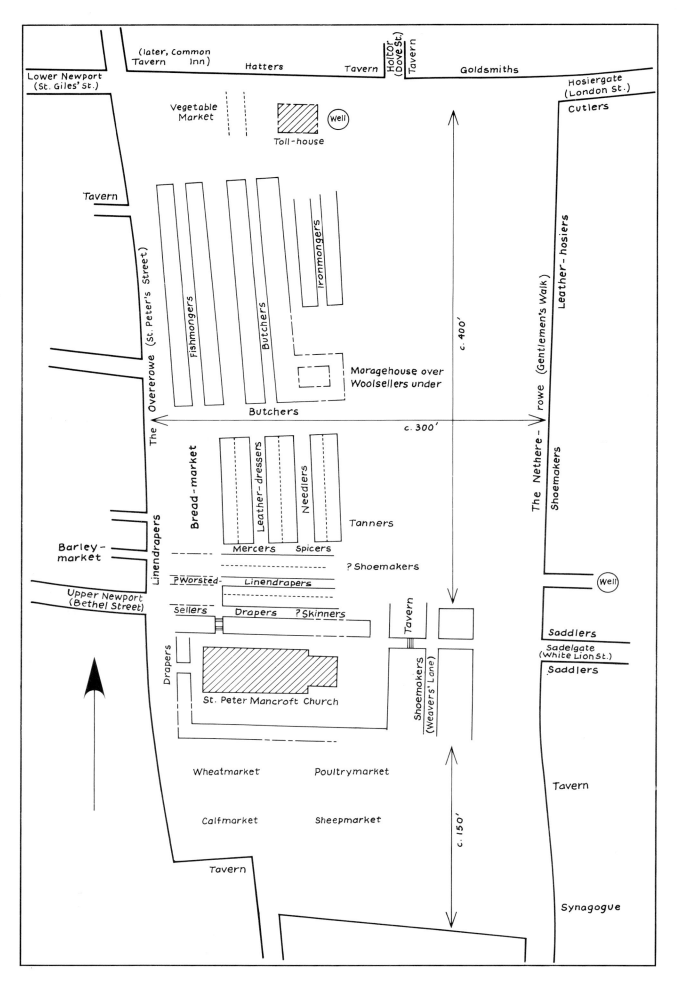

The medieval Market, 1300–1500

IN medieval times by far the greater part of all buying and selling was carried on at fairs and town markets. Unlike fairs, which were annual or bi-annual events often associated with religious festivals, markets were held regularly, usually weekly or twice weekly, to meet the needs of the local community. Norwich market-days, on Mancroft, were on Wednesdays and Saturdays, except for a time around 1300, when there seems to have been a daily market.

In 1300, the provision Market and its various subsidiary markets covered a vast area, stretching from what is now the line of Guildhall Hill and London Street almost as far as St Stephens church. The huge space devoted to trading reflected the pre-eminence of Norwich as a provincial capital and an inland port. With an estimated population of between 6,000 and 10,000, the city was one of the biggest and richest towns in the country, and it was set in one of the most thickly peopled regions of medieval England. The Market needed to be large. Grain and wool, cattle, sheep, and poultry from the productive acres of East Anglia were brought there for sale, as well as the many and varied manufactures of the city's leather, cloth, and metal workers, and the foreign imports landed by the merchants at the riverside staithes.

Cattle, sheep, and poultry were sold in the open space to the south of St Peter Mancroft church, and horses near St Stephens. (An echo of this earlier role can be found in the present-day name of Rampant Horse Street, which derives from an inn that once stood near the Horse Market.) The Swine Market had been separate from an early date; it was held originally at All Saints Green and then on Hog Hill (now Orford Hill), not far from the Timber Market, which gave its name to Timber Hill. Just off the main market-place was the Maddermarket, where dye for the weaving industry was sold.

In the main market-place to the north of St Peter Mancroft, as the map shows, the higher ground between the church and the Tollhouse was occupied by 'rows' of the permanent stalls of the meat and fish sellers, and the shops and stalls of the woollen and linen drapers. A range of substantial buildings in front of the meat market housed more shops and also the 'Murage Loft', used for the collection of the tolls levied after 1294 for the erection of the city's stone walls, which replaced the earlier earthen bank.

Other areas in the open market and round its periphery were allotted to particular crafts and trades. The disproportionate amount of space given over to craftsmen associated with leather-working – tanners, skinners, cordwainers, saddlers, and gaiter-makers –

Norwich provision Market, c.1300; drawn by Margot Tillyard (not to scale).

is especially interesting, since it underlines the predominance of the leather industry in Norwich at this period.

The shops and stalls varied in size and form. They could be as wide as 15 ft. or as narrow as 2 ft. – the latter the measurement of a basket-stand in the bakery. Some of the shops are described in property deeds as forming part of sizeable buildings with rooms (or 'solars') above them and cellars beneath. Others, especially round the perimeter, were lean-to structures which in time became permanent, leaving the properties behind to be reached from the street. The row of houses still to be seen today below St Peter's churchyard and bordering Weavers' Lane marks the site of the old Shoemakers' Row. Plots for these shops were first released by the city authorities around 1300.

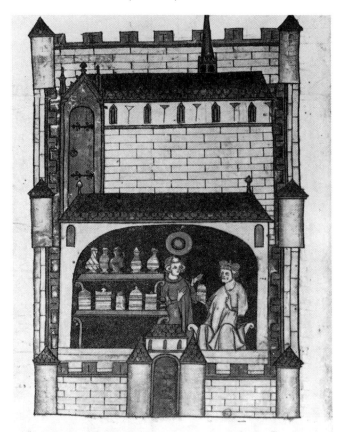

An apothecary's shop. French c.1300.
(By permission of the British Library)

The market shops and stalls changed hands like other items of real estate. They were highly profitable investments in a great city like Norwich, generating a useful income from rents, and ground landlords were often large and prosperous institutions such as fraternities and other religious bodies, craft gilds and charities. This was a period when there was a strong

Shops, fifteenth century. From left to right: a draper's, a furrier's, a barber's, and a grocer's. French.

demand for shops and intense activity in market property. The Norwich bailiffs (then the city's rulers) were able to augment the civic revenues by allowing many more stalls to be built in the market-place in exchange for perpetual rent.

The open expanse below the market 'rows' – known as the 'Lower Market' and later as the 'Great Market' – was kept clear of permanent building for the use of the country smallholders who brought their produce for sale on market-days. They would have crammed all available space with an untidy jumble of carts, booths, and tents, interspersed with the pitches of those who had come by packhorse, carrying their goods in deep semicircular baskets ('peds') slung either side of the saddle, and laying them out on the dirt floor of the market-place.

The press of people, animals, and wagons must have brought about acute congestion, since the pattern of narrow lanes and alleys leading in and out of the market-place is likely to have changed little since the days of the Conquest. 'Saddlegate' (White Lion Street) was the principal link with the Castle, and probably also provided the main access from the important thoroughfares of Ber Street and St Stephens Street, while 'Holtor' (Dove Street) was the only direct approach road from the north. The more imposing highways of 'Upper and Lower Newport' (St Giles Street and Bethel Street) led in from the west, but on the east, 'Hosiergate' (London Street), meandering around the Castle Ditches, can hardly have been a main line of communication. Vehicular access to the market-place must have been restricted and difficult – as indeed it was to remain for many centuries.

In its early days the Mancroft Market, like most fairs and markets, was held under licence from the King, since the right to trade and receive revenues was part of the royal prerogative. But it was a privilege that the sovereign was often prepared to bestow on a town or institution in return for a sum of money or a special service or favour. Norwich acquired the control of its Market through the benefice of Edward III. Most opportunely, the King's visit to stage a jousting tournament in 1341 coincided with the completion and fortification of the city walls – built, as the authorities put it, 'for the profit and defence of the city and adjacent county and for the honour of the King'. Much pleased with Norwich and encouraged by his mother Queen Isobel, Edward made handsome recompense for the heavy costs of the building work by granting the franchise of the Market to the city's rulers in perpetuity. From then on all proceeds from tolls and the dues paid by stallholders went into the city's coffers, and the King's Clerk ceased to exercise jurisdiction over the trade there.

Once they held the operating franchise, the Norwich bailiffs could frame their own ordinances for local trading. Like all marketing regulations in medieval England these were complex and comprehensive. Rightful municipal revenue had to be protected from toll evasion. Moreover, it was vital to make sure that scarce commodities were distributed as fairly as possible, because deprivation could so easily detonate disorder and riot among urban populations unable to support themselves. To give everyone a fair start, no edible goods could be sold on Norwich Market until the Cathedral bell had tolled for Lady Mass (i.e. 6 a.m.). As elsewhere, off-market trading and attempts at profiteering were severely discouraged: no-one must hide goods in houses or yards with a view to avoiding the toll, nor must anyone go to meet goods coming into the city by road or water, thus hindering their free sale in the Market. This practice was known as 'forestalling' and was a grave offence, since it enabled middlemen to corner the market and 'engross' or force up the price. What would now be called retail trading – buying to sell at a profit – was restricted to merchants who had paid their dues as Freemen of the city and were therefore regarded as contributing to the general good of the community. But the temptation to trade on the most favourable terms regardless of the ordinances was very strong; the many indictments brought before the Norwich courts show how often the rules were flouted.

There were constant disagreements about weights and measures, not only because deliberately selling short was a common offence but also because, in the absence of nationally accepted standards, variations between one town and another led to genuine misunderstandings. In Norwich there was strict control of weights and measures from an early date. The city's 'Custumal' (Book of Customs, or by-laws), of 1308, laid down that measures used by the merchants must be examined several times a year and marked with the city's seal, unless found to be false, in which case they were destroyed. The prices of the staple commodities of bread and ale were fixed locally and were known as the Assize; but Norwich bakers and alewives, like their fellows elsewhere, seemed to contravene the Assize almost as a matter of course, and might expect a session in the stocks if they could not pay the fine.

The city's early fourteenth-century prosperity, of which the increase in the number of market stalls is good evidence, received a severe setback in 1349 with the terrible visitation of the Black Death, which took an enormous toll of traders and customers alike. Many hundreds died. Inevitably, there were changes in the Market in consequence. A few years after the epidemic it was recorded that many stalls were ruinous and without tenants; and when famine followed plague in 1369, the urgent need for extra burial space led to the enlargement of St Peter Mancroft churchyard by the sweeping away of the drapery and linen-drapery stalls.

However, within less than a decade there were signs that the city's basic resilience was leading to a strong recovery. The merchant community, rich and prosperous, were a powerful influence in city government and – probably at their instigation – the council again sought to increase civic holdings of market property. By 1397 the city had acquired many more shops and stalls. About the same time the staithes on the river in King Street were also bought up and a direction issued that all goods coming into Norwich by water must be landed there. These were measures designed not only to increase revenues, but also to tighten the monopoly of the local merchants.

The old market Tollhouse was still the headquarters of civic government in the early fifteenth century, although it had become hopelessly inadequate for the needs of local administration and, moreover, could no longer be considered worthy of a thriving and proud borough. Its deficiencies were even more obvious after 1404, when the ruling oligarchy secured a new royal charter granting the city the rights of full incorporation with the status of 'The County of the City of Norwich'. Only three years later work was begun on a suitably prestigious Guildhall. It was one of the grandest outside London, and was intended to accommodate all departments of civil administration and justice, which, after 1404, were the dual responsibility of the reconstituted governing body, now headed by a Mayor, Sheriffs, and Aldermen. The old Murage Loft, superfluous since the walls had been completed, took over the tax and excise functions of the Tollhouse and became the office where tolls were paid and the market-supervisor sat. The Mayor himself was now Clerk of the Markets, *ex officio*, but the work was always carried out by a deputy.

The medieval Guildhall in 1845, before later nineteenth-century alterations.
(Local Studies Library)

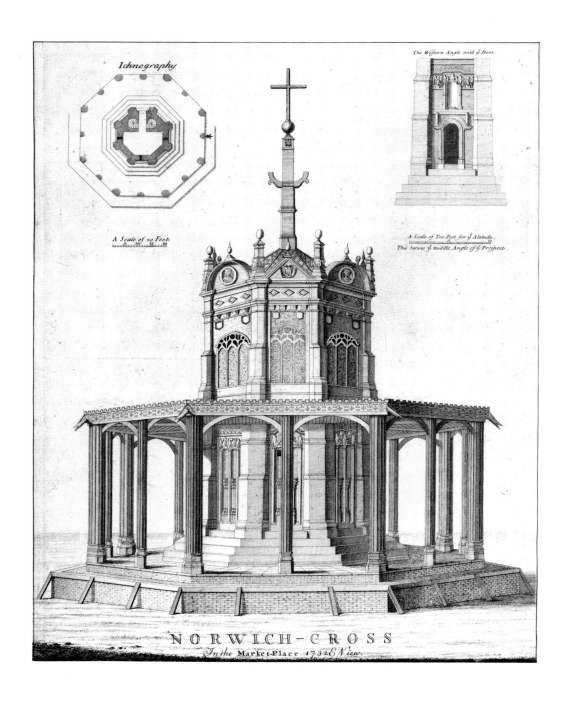

Ichnography

A Scale of 20 Feet

The Western Angle with ý Door.

A Scale of Ten Feet for ý Altitude.
This Serves ý middle Angle of ý Prospect.

NORWICH-CROSS
In the Market-Place 1732 E View.

The Market Cross

This print by Sheldrake is dated 1730. It was probably made shortly before the Cross was demolished.
(Norfolk Museums Service)

AFTER the Guildhall, the Cross must have been the most striking architectural feature in the medieval Market. It stood as a centrepiece in the Lower Market, opposite what is now Davey Place. We know little about the first recorded Cross, erected soon after the grant of the market franchise to the city by Edward III. But its successor, built between 1501 and 1503 by Mayor John Rightwise, was a graceful structure reaching 60 to 70 ft. and standing on a 30 ft. wide plinth. This Cross, with various alterations and additions, adorned the market-place for 230 years.

The Cross originally contained a central chapel or oratory, occupied by an officiating priest. But at the

Reformation, when the rood group on the pinnacle was torn down and the chapel converted into a storehouse, the Cross lost its spiritual significance and became purely utilitarian. In fact, by the seventeenth century it seems to have been more often called the Market House than the Cross. Grain and other commodities sold by the bushel were traded there, since the approved measures with the city's coat of arms were kept chained to the pillars for anyone to use; and the octagonal arcade served as a shelter for successive generations of vendors and customers. The area round the Cross was a favourite place for the itinerant sellers of small wares and fancy goods to display their merchandise, and overcrowding sometimes led to intervention from the Mayor's Court with instructions that pitches must be moved elsewhere.

The official with the impressive title of 'Keeper of the Cross' was actually the humble market-sweeper – a very necessary appointment in view of the amount of refuse, and in particular the prodigious heaps of horse droppings generated on market-days. It can hardly have been an easy task. The incumbent in the 1670s, one John Buddwell, was required to clear not only the market-place, but also the city's four bridges, as well as several areas of waste ground, for an annual wage of £8 10s; if he failed to sweep the Market once a week and the rest once a fortnight 5s was stopped from his pay; and he was threatened with dismissal if muck made at the Saturday Market was still there on the following Tuesday. But the problem was constant and ever-increasing. It would not really be solved until the advent of petrol-driven transport.

The Cross was expensive to maintain and over the years the citizens were repeatedly taxed to raise funds for its repair and beautification, especially when distinguished visitors were expected. So it is all the more sad that in 1732 the interests of commerce allied to civic miserliness evidently overcame civic pride. The Cross was ruthlessly pulled down, the stone sold for £125, and the site levelled. There seems to have been surprisingly little protest at the time.

A city whiffler in front of the Guildhall.
(Norfolk Museums Service)

Ceremonial, celebration, & spectacle, 1500–1700

THE importance of the market-place to the city and its inhabitants went far beyond its purely commercial function, since for many centuries it played a vital role in the popular culture of the community. Within the scope of this booklet it would be impossible to cover fully this vivid and varied aspect of market life over such a wide time-span, and we have chosen to represent it with examples from sixteenth- and seventeenth-century Norwich.

Even as late as 1700 the Great Market was still unencumbered with permanent stalls so that, except on market-days, it was available as a huge public space, providing a natural arena for all kinds of communal activity. It was the focus for traditional pageantry and celebration; the place where the largely illiterate population would gather to hear pronouncements by the Mayor on matters of national and local importance; a recreation ground where they could find diversion and free entertainment on public holidays and royal occasions; and, at times, a battle ground for popular riot and affray.

Until the middle years of the sixteenth century, when the Reformation abruptly changed and curtailed communal religious observance, ritual and ceremonial lay at the heart of all social activity. This was particularly true of urban communities. The citizen's year revolved round the perennial festivals of the Catholic calendar, each marked by its special ceremonies and usually a public procession. Although such assemblies centred on the parish churches, the market-place would surely have been the scene of much of the open-air pageantry associated with them.

We know that the great procession of the craft gilds at Corpus Christi – perhaps the most significant and solemn occasion in the city's year in the early sixteenth century – began with a perambulation of the market-place. This was pageantry in which the majority of the working population could join – either walking with their craft companies wearing distinctive gowns in colours chosen to match those corresponding London Livery Company, or participating as actors in the wagon-mounted mystery plays which were an essential part of the proceedings. There is little doubt that the Mysteries would have been performed in the market-place as well as at other stations in the town.

After the Reformation much of the mystical element of public celebration was lost; and, with the disbandment of many of the craft gilds which followed it, the rituals of Corpus Christi lapsed. One consequence was that direct involvement of the working population in city pageantry, which had been so much a part of medieval life, practically ceased. They became spectators rather than participants.

This does not mean that the people's love of ceremonial was in any way diminished. From the fifteenth century until well into the nineteenth, the most popular event in the civic calendar was the inauguration of the newly elected Mayor in May of each year. This was an extravagant spectacle staged, some may have thought, as a reaffirmation of the overbearing authority of Mayor and Aldermen. But for the multitude gathered in front of the garlanded Guildhall to await the arrival of the new Mayor and his retinue and to hear his speech to the citizens, it was a magnificent public show. Nevertheless, despite its carnival trappings, the Mayor's inauguration retained a strong religious element, since it was combined with the ceremonial of the surviving and powerful Gild of St George.

The new and old Mayors rode side by side on splendidly caparisoned horses, followed by the Court in their robes of justice – the Aldermen in scarlet, the Sheriffs in violet, gowns. They were preceded by trumpeters, and standard-bearers carrying the flags of England and St George. Alongside walked the City Waits, clad in their blue cloaks and silver chains of

On countless historic and royal occasions the market-place was the scene of communal rejoicing and sorrow. The mourning procession on the death of Henry VIII was followed soon afterwards by the pageantry celebrating Edward VI's coronation. A large effigy of Solomon led the parade, symbolizing the wisdom of the nine-year-old King; free ale was plentifully available; and an incongruous mermaid diverted the crowds. In 1578, Queen Elizabeth crossed the 'goodly garnished' market-place en route to her lodging at the Bishop's Palace and the heart-felt but interminable orations of her loyal Norwich subjects. She rode past the specially redecorated Cross and between the ranks of the craft companies, lined up in their liveries to greet her. When Charles II arrived at the Guildhall in 1671 to view the panorama

A standard-bearer.
(*Norfolk Museums Service*)

The dragon.
(*Norfolk Museums Service*)

office, to play the procession through the streets, and ahead four 'Whifflers' cleared a path, skilfully brandishing dangerous-looking swords. But for the spectators the favourites must surely have been the dragon – its flapping wings and turning head drawing a frisson of mock terror from those nearest the route – and the clown-like 'Dick Fools' in their traditional gowns of red and yellow ornamented with cats' tails and bells, who waved small wands in imitation of the Whifflers. Inauguration day was an event eagerly awaited by townsfolk and country visitors alike.

of the city from its balcony, he looked down on the entire city regiment ranged in the market-place in their red coats. According to the Town Clerk, the King was hailed by 'the reiterated acclamations of joy from the people, who soe filled the whole market-place as his majesty's coach had scarce room to pass'.

National triumphs, military victories, coronations, and royal birthdays were celebrated in the market-place with dancing round blazing bonfires, the firing of volleys by the assembled militia, fireworks, and a jangle of bells from all the surrounding churches, while those living in houses round the Market were expected to contribute to the festive atmosphere by setting lighted candles in their windows. Mayoral largesse in the form of free beer was customary on such occasions which, not surprisingly, tended to degenerate into rowdy and unrestrained Bacchanalia. It was common, especially in the eighteenth century, for immense triumphal arches to be erected beside the Guildhall to acknowledge particularly momentous events. Although temporary and of a flimsy construction, these must have been a frustrating hindrance to market traffic.

There were also wild scenes in the market-place at the time of Norfolk Parliamentary elections. Excited

Dick Fool
(Norfolk Museums Service)

partisans crowded round the Cross, which was the centre of the proceedings, their numbers swollen by cartloads of country voters brought in by the candidates to ensure good support, and provided with free board and lodging. Lavish bribes of liquor were guaranteed to fuel their fervour. When all the inns were full, the crowds spilled over into the market-place, sleeping in and around the Cross 'like flocks of sheep', as Sir Thomas Browne described them in 1679. This election was a particularly contentious affair – a battle between early Whigs and Tories at the height of the Exclusion crisis. The Mayor's Court took no chances. Every parish constable was ordered to appear personally at the Cross at 8 a.m., armed with his staff, to help prevent or suppress 'disorder and tumult by turbulent persons'. They were in for a long day; carousal, insults, and fighting were likely to continue long after votes had been counted and the

The triumphal arch erected to honour the Duke of Cumberland after he had quelled the Jacobite rebellion in 1745. The panels were painted on silk, made transparent by hundreds of lights inside the arch.
(Norfolk Museums Service)

victorious candidate chaired 'thrice round the market', accompanied by trumpeters and torch-bearers.

There were more sombre happenings. The market-place was the stage for public punishments of all degrees of severity. Stocks and a pillory stood at the eastern end of the Guildhall, prominently placed to invite the taunts of passers-by. The stocks were used for a variety of relatively minor offences, from brawling with neighbours and breaking the Assize to railing at the magistrates and behaving rudely towards the Mayor.

Other punishments were more brutal. In the 1550s and 1560s men convicted of 'the speaking of seditious words' were committed to be 'set upon the pillory with both ears nailed to the same'. After this treatment the ears were cut off and the accused thrown into gaol. Infringements of the moral code of the day were dealt with harshly. One offender, found guilty in the 1550s of 'the abominable vice of whoredom', and considered unreformed after a session in the stocks, was sentenced to be carried about the market-place with a symbolic hood upon his head to expose him to public ridicule; his partner, meanwhile, was set in the stocks. Persistent culprits guilty of this offence might be 'whipped round the market', a punishment that meant lashing until the blood flowed. As late as 1669, the Mayor's Court minutes record the appointment

The whipping of a vagrant.
(From Holinshed's Chronicles, 1577. By permission of the British Library)

of a 'whipper, basket-carrier, brander and hangman'. (It is fairly safe to assume that the basket was for the carting away of muck).

The hangman, certainly, was no stranger to the Market. Hangings were commonplace and were not always recorded, so that no-one knows how many met their death in this way. But we do know that gallows were set up at the Cross for the mass execution of 60 of Kett's rebels after Warwick's superior forces had recaptured the market-place and crushed the 1549 insurrection. Much later, in 1674, the exemplary hanging took place at the same spot of young Thomas Berney, the son of a former High Sheriff of Norfolk, who had killed a companion with a sword-thrust following a drunken brawl during Assize Week. This was a shocking and much publicized affair. In the bald words of a contemporary pamphlet: 'He was carried to the common place of execution where . . . he suffered according to the law, his body was put into a coffin and delivered to his friends to inter'.

Other spectacles in the seventeenth-century Market, although less cruelly merciless than a public hanging, were scarcely less macabre. Human deformities were regarded as legitimate entertainment, and the Mayor's Court had no qualms about issuing licences to the many travelling showmen anxious to make money from the exhibition of unfortunates with grotesque physical abnormalities. In the 1670s and 1680s permission was granted for displays involving, for example: 'a monstrous hayrie child'; 'a girl of sixteen with no bones'; 'a child with six fingers on each hand and six toes on each foot'; 'a little dwarf of 37 years of age'; 'a monstrous man taken from amongst the hills of Corinthia, he feeds on the roots of trees etc'; 'a monstrous man with 2 bodies brought

from the Indies by Sir Thomas Grantham'; and 'a German woman born without arms and hands and does extraordinary things. She doth marvellous things with her feet'.

There were plenty of shows of a lighter kind in the seventeenth century. Exotic animals were a constant source of wonder; and lions, camels, dancing bears, elephants, a monkey, tigers, and jackals appeared at various times in the market-place or in near-by inns. Licences were issued to acrobats, rope-dancers (one of whom performed on crutches), exponents of sleight-of-hand, fire-eaters, puppeteers, and ballad-singers. Quacks and mountebanks selling drugs and patent remedies were sure to draw large crowds, especially those 'doctors' who promised to perform miraculous cures in public view. Their huge stages (one as large as 16 ft. long and 30 ft. wide) cluttered up the 'Hall's End', drawing periodic complaints from the fishmongers that they could not reach their stalls. At times the Mayor's Court took fright in case the size of the crowds became a threat to public order; and one popular visitor, 'Doctor' Cornelius Tilbourne, had his licence hastily withdrawn because of possible damage to the city's economy by the distraction of 'idle minds' from their work.

Looking towards the Walk from the 'Library Opening' (now the Advice Arcade), undated, probably mid-nineteenth century.
(Norfolk Museums Service)

The Coaching Age

IN the seventeenth and eighteenth centuries the improving condition of major roads and the growth of coach travel brought increasing numbers of visitors to Norwich, boosting the trade of the Market and its encircling fringe of shops. The country gentry of Norfolk and Suffolk, with their womenfolk, found it easier to reach the city and they took to coming more often and for longer periods, attracted by a round of fashionable social events and leisure diversions second only to those found in London or in resort towns such as Bath. Shops and services multiplied to cater for their custom. By the second half of the seventeenth century the old barriers to retail selling were coming down and Norwich traders were not slow to rise to the challenge. Superior shops geared to gentry tastes and pursuits, such as mercers and milliners, booksellers, vintners, confectioners, wigmakers, and gunsmiths, were established round the market-place, especially along its eastern edge where the most imposing houses were.

The size and magnificence of the Market greatly impressed late seventeenth-century visitors. Thomas Baskerville wrote in 1681:

A little way from this castle on the opposite side of a hill, is the chief market place of this city, and this being the only place where all things are brought to be sold for the food for this great city, they not as in London allowing markets in several places, make it vastly full of provisions, especially on Saturdays, where I saw the greatest shambles for butchers' meat I had ever yet seen, and the like also for poultry and dairy meats, which dairy people also bring many quarters of veal with their butter and cheese, and I believe also in their seasons pork and hog-meats. These people fill a square of ground on the side of a hill as big as Abingdon market place. They setting their goods in ranges as may be one above another, only allowing room for single persons to pass between: and above these the butchers have their shambles and such kind of people as sell fish, of which there are plenty of such kinds as the seas hereabouts afford. viz. crabs, flounders, mackerel, very cheap, but lobster for sea-fish and pike or jack for river fish, were dear enough. They asked me for one pike under 2 foot, 2s 6d., and for a pot of pickled oysters they would have a shilling.

One consequence of the gentry invasion was the transformation of the old 'Nether Row' – or the lowest street of the Market – into a favourite promenade for the social elite, earning it the sobriquet 'Gentlemen's Walk'. It was, as Baskerville described it, 'a fair Walk before the prime inns and houses of the market-place . . . called gentlemen's walk or walking place . . . kept clear for the purpose from the encumbrance of stalls, tradesmen and their goods'. In its early days the Walk was no more than a kerbless pathway and keeping it free from market impedimenta was easier said

*The market-place in 1806: a lithograph by H. Ninham
from a water colour by J.S. Cotman. This famous view
tends to make the market-place look even larger than it was.
The meat and fish markets are hidden behind the tall
buildings on the right. The Walk is on the left.*
(Norfolk Museums Service)

than done; on one occasion eminent members of the Market Committee turned out in person to remove traders' baskets. But throughout the eighteenth century and well into the nineteenth, it remained the most popular place in the city for those with leisure to congregate – to stroll, to gossip, to window-shop, to see and be seen. The 'interesting characters' encountered there in 1800 by the Rev. J. Larwood were probably a representative cross-section: 'the merchant, the manufacturer, the magistrate, the provincial yeoman, the militia officer, the affluent landlord, the thrifty and thriving tenant, the independent farmer, the recruiting officer, the clergy faculty, barristers, and all the various characters of polished and professional society'.

By this time the topography of the medieval market-place had altered, although by no means as drastically as it would in the twentieth century. Encroachment of domestic building into the market space was never as extensive as it was in many other towns. Nevertheless, by the seventeenth century, the row which had contained the old Murage House (see map on p.8) had become an almost continuous range of three- and four-storeyed buildings stretching right across the main market-place from north to south and another row of tall houses running east/west extended up the hill in front of St Peter's church. The Great Market was thus effectively cut off from the 'Upper Market' which housed the meat and fish stalls, although wheeled traffic had access to the latter via Guildhall Hill. Otherwise, only two narrow passages linked the two sections of the Market. (One of these survives as the flight of steps next to St Peter's churchyard still known as Pudding Lane.) There were advantages in this segregation. The malodorous rows of the Shambles and the Fish Market were now hidden in decent obscurity from the main market area and the eyes, if not the noses, of the fashionable promenaders along the Walk were spared offence.

By the end of the seventeenth century the congestion caused by the herds of cattle, flocks of sheep, and strings of wagoners' carts driven into the St Peter Mancroft area had become intolerable and efforts were being made to find a more open site. Eventually, parts of the banks and ditches of the Castle defences were levelled on the eastern side of the mound and in 1738 the weekly livestock sales were transferred to what is now known as the old Cattle Market, where they continued to be held until the 1960s. The Hay Market remained on the old site – perpetuating the name – until the early nineteenth century, when the ancient hay-weighing machine was moved to a custom-built house on the new livestock market.

A vast and varied trade was transacted on the Great Market and in the early 1700s a committee was formed to lessen the burden of the Clerk of the Markets. The following extracts from the minute-books of the 1720s show not only the range of

Norwich Market Place, by Thomas Rowlandson, 1788.
Pudding Lane is seen in the centre of the picture and on the right of it is one of the few groups of seventeenth- and eighteenth-century buildings that still survive.
(Norfolk Museums Service)

merchandise offered for sale, but also the manner in which it was sold. The list is not exhaustive; the notes of John Kirkpatrick, the antiquarian, who was a member of the committee, show that other goods such as brooms and besoms, pattens and baskets, plough-wheels and horse-collars, were among the divers items that could be bought there.

Account of the severall articles collected by the Deputy Clerk of the Lower Market for eatables and other things brought there to be sold and what each person pay weekly or quarterly

8 May 1721

Every pedde [basket] of fruit one penny a weeke
Every Gardiner 2 pence a weeke or 2s a quarter
Fogger [dealer] selling porke 2s a quarter or 2 pence a with a stoole. But if only pedde 2d a weeke
For persons selling soap 2s a quarter 2d a weeke
For persons selling Hatts & Books or Bundles 2s a quarter or 2d a weeke
For persons selling Oat Meale, salt, flower or meal one shilling a quarter for every killer [tub]
For every person that hawk the markett with laces or garters or Ballades or pamphlets one penny a week each
Every Ginger Bread stall 2s a quarter or 2d a weeke
For all persons selling pattens 2d a week
For all persons selling earthenware on the ground 2s a week
All fish carts 4s each
Every swill [basket] of fish 1d except a Peddar [pedlar] load out of it then the Peddar pay
For every country butcher selling meat Wednesday or Saturday sixpence a peice each day
For the Yarmouth Gardiners 2d for every tubb
Every cart of pease & beans, turnips, carrotts, parsnips, pears, apples, onions or any such like herbage each cart 4d.
For every horse load of pease or beans or apples, pears, carrotts, turnips, parsnips tho in peds or sacks 1 penny

August, 1721

John Ebbotts has leave to sell rabbits 2s a year. He is to have the liberty of the Hall porch in rainy weather.

8 July, 1724

Kidder [dealer in farm produce] bringing peds into the market with butter cheese etc shall pay 1d for every market day
And such as use stools for pork, puddings, links [sausages] or other provisions 2d for every stool besides a 1d for their peds
That every City Gardiner pay 2d for their standing with stall every Saturday and 1d for any other market day the rest of the week for nothing
And that every particular person selling fruit or other garden ware shall pay 1d every market day.
And that the Orange people [Dutch] pay the same with the Gardiners
Salt carts 2s a quarter or be removed

With the huge growth in coaching traffic the inns round the market-place assumed a new importance. For at least the next century they were to play a central role in all aspects of the commercial and social life of

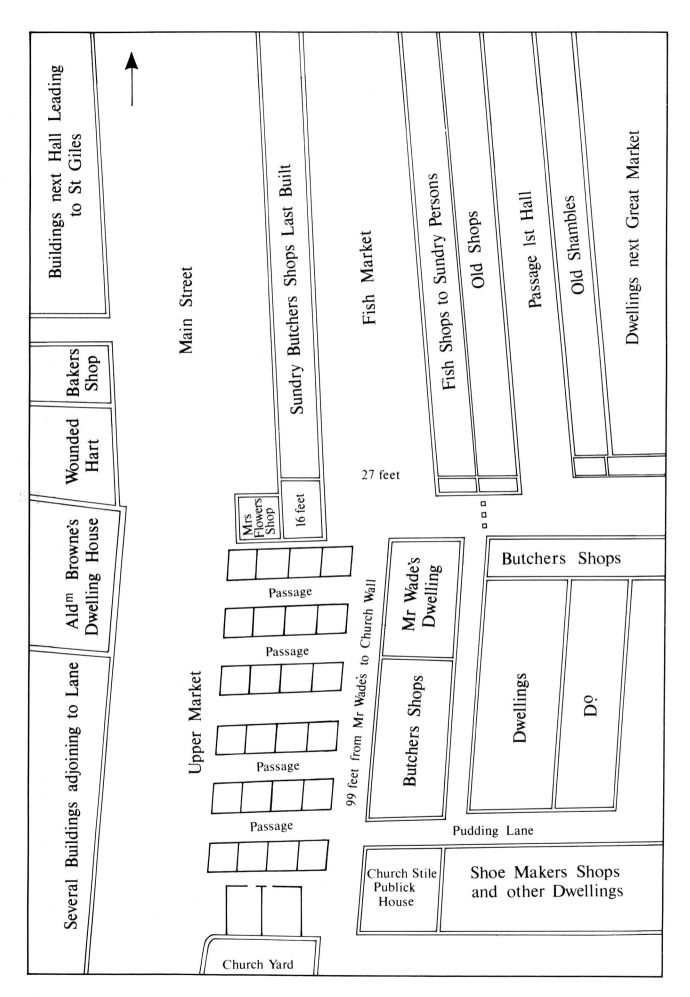

Buildings next Hall Leading to St Giles

Bakers Shop

Wounded Hart

Ald^m Browne's Dwelling House

Several Buildings adjoining to Lane

Main Street

Sundry Butchers Shops Last Built

Fish Market

Fish Shops to Sundry Persons

Old Shops

Passage 1st Hall

Old Shambles

Dwellings next Great Market

Mrs Flowers Shop

16 feet

27 feet

Passage

Passage

Upper Market

Passage

Passage

Passage

99 feet from Mr Wade's to Church Wall

Mr Wade's Dwelling

Butchers Shops

Butchers Shops

Dwellings

D^o.

Pudding Lane

Church Stile Publick House

Shoe Makers Shops and other Dwellings

Church Yard

the city, serving not only as hostelries, but also as business premises and sale-rooms, warehouses, play-houses, concert-halls and club-rooms, masonic lodges, post offices, and long-distance coach stations.

At least four large inns opened on to the Walk between 'Cockey Lane' (the old 'Hosiergate', now London Street) and White Lion Lane. Their narrow gateways led into long yards overlooked by the galleries that gave access to the guest rooms on the first and second floors. Grouped round the yard on the ground floor were the public rooms – the 'ordinary', where a fixed-price meal could be had, the warehouses used by itinerant dealers for the storage and sale of their stock, club-rooms and auction-rooms for hire, and the card- and gambling-rooms (well patronised despite the fact that gambling was unlawful and if discovered could lose the landlord his licence). At the further end of the yard were the stables, the hay and fodder lofts, and lodging for grooms and ostlers; and below were the cellars and vaults amply stocked with supplies of beer and imported wines. There was access at the far end of the yard to the passage known as Back of the Inns, but this tortuous and noisome alley was not wide enough to take carriage traffic.

Most famous of the inns along the Walk was the

A curiously inanimate sketch of the Angel Yard by Edward Pocock. Although dated 1761, this drawing was made in the nineteenth century, evidently copied from an earlier version.
(Local Studies Library)

Angel, dating from the fifteenth century. In Ninham's lithograph on p.18 a coach and horses can be seen driving into its gateway, now the entrance to the Royal Arcade. Over many years the Angel played host to innumerable showmen, acrobats, animal handlers, and performers of all kinds, and in the seventeenth century its yard was popular as an auditorium with some of the many companies of strolling players to visit Norwich – always an important centre of theatrical activity, even though the city did not acquire a purpose-built playhouse until 1758. But the Angel's reputation as a fashionable theatre was seriously damaged when disaster struck in 1699; the gallery collapsed while Mr Thomas Doggett's renowned company of players was entertaining a full house, killing a young woman and injuring many other people. Despite repairs, confi-dence of audiences never altogether returned and after the accident the Angel yard was used only for puppet shows and similar events and never again for full-scale theatrical performances.

The King's Head (or the King's Arms), on the site of what is now Davey Place, was another ancient and popular hostelry. In the 1680s the landlady, widow Berne, was noted for the 'very good ordinary' which she served on Saturdays and Thomas Baskerville reported dining there in the congenial company of

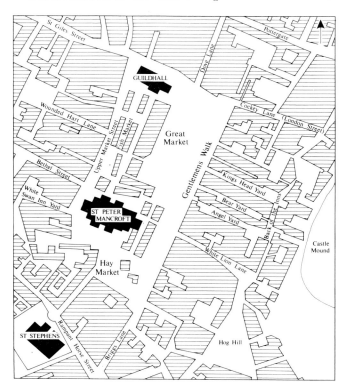

The centre of the city in 1789, taken from the map by Anthony Hochstetter. Note the inn-yards on the right.

21

Yarmouth Divifion.

George Wymer, Gent. No. 42, St. Giles's Broad-ftreet, for the town of Great Yarmouth, the hundreds of Holt, North and South Erpingham, Tunftead, Happing, Eaft and Weft Flegg.

Lynn Divifion.

Wm. Money, Gent. of Holkham, Norfolk, for the Borough of Lynn Regis, Freebridge Lynn and Marfhland, Smithdon, Clackclofe, Gallow, Brothercrofs, North and South Greenhoe, and Grimfhoe

Thetford Divifion.

Rifhton Woodcocke, Gent. No. 5, White-lion-lane, for the town of Thetford, (Norfolk Side) the Hundreds of Earfham, Eynsford, Humble-yard, Forehoe, Difs, Shropham, Giltcrofs, Mitford, Launditch, and Wayland

---

STAGE COACHES, DILIGENCES, WAGGONS and BARGE to and from NORWICH.

The Old NORWICH MACHINE,
By NEWMARKET, in one Day.

From the Maid's Head in St. Simon's, Norwich, every Sunday, Tuefday and Thurfday night, at ten o'clock; and from the Bull Inn, Bifhopgate-ftreet, London, every Monday, Wednefday and Friday night, at the fame hour, at 15s. each, 14lb. luggage allowed.

LONDON and NORWICH EXPEDITION.

From the fame Inns; fets out from Norwich every Monday, Wednefday and Friday evenings at ten, and from London every Sunday, Tuefday, and Thurfday at the fame time; carries four infide paffengers, at 18s. each, outfides 10s. 6d. 14lb. luggage allowed, all above three halfpence per pound.

The above coaches carry game on the following terms, viz. a hare 6d. brace of pheafants 6d. and brace of partridges 3d.

The POST COACH, from the Angel in the Market-place, Norwich.
By Diss, Bury, Sudbury, and Chelmsford.

Comes down every Monday, Wednefday and Friday, and goes up every Tuefday, Thurfday and Saturday. Infides 15s. Outfids 10s. 6d.

A MACHINE COACH, in one Day, from the Angel,
By way of Needham, Coddock, Colchester. and Chelmsford.

Sets out from Norwich every Sunday, Tuefday, and Thurfday evenings at ten, and from London every Monday, Wednefday and Friday evenings, at the fame hour. Infides 15s. Outfides 10s. 6d.

The PARTIE CARREE,
By Bury and Sudbury, carries four infides only, at 18s. each.

From the Angel, in Norwich, every Sunday, Wednefday, and Friday morning, and from London every Tuefday, Thurfday, and Saturday mornings precifely at four o'clock, and gets in about 8 in the evening. During the winter feafon it travels in a Day and Half, fetting out from Norwich every Tuefday, Thurfday and Saturday, at one o'clock in the afternoon, refts at Bury, and proceeds the next morning for London. From London this coach fets out the fame days at eight in the morning, refts at Bury, and finifhes its journey the next day before dinner.

The

The DILIGENCE and New POST-COACH.

From the King's Head in the Market-place, in and out every day (alternately) to the White Horfe in Fetter-lane, London, fets out at each precifely at ten o'clock. The Diligence carries three paffengers only, the Poft-Coach four, at 1l. 1s. each, allowed 14lb. luggage, and three halfpence per lb. for parcels by weight. A guard attends the carriages in and out of London.

The NORWICH MERCURY.

From the Swan in St. Peter's Mancroft, fets out on Sunday, Tuefday and Thurfday nights at fix o'clock, to the Plough Inn, Princes-ftreet, Soho, London, by way of Bury and Sudbury, and gets into London in time for the Bath coach; returns from thence every Monday, Wednefday and Friday evening at nine o'clock; carries five infides only, at 1l. 1s. each, allowed 12lb. luggage, all above three halfpence per lb.

LYNN and NORWICH DILIGENCE.
In Eight Hours, by way of Swaffham and Dereham.

Sets out from the White Lion in Lynn, both fummer and winter, every Monday, Wednefday and Friday morning at eight o'clock, to the White Swan in St. Peter's Mancroft, Norwich, and arrives in time for the Yarmouth coach of that day, during the fummer feafon; returns from the Swan every Tuefday, Thurfday and Saturday morning at the fame hour. It carries three infide paffengers at 12s. each, and 14lb. luggage allowed; outfides half price. Short paffengers at 3d. halfpenny per mile.

The LYNN DILIGENCE.

From the King's Head in the Market-place, Norwich, to the Crown in Lynn, every Monday, Wednefday and Friday morning, and returns from Lynn every Tuefday, Thurfday and Saturday mornings, at eight o'clock. Paffengers at 12s. each, and 14lb. luggage allowed; outfides half price.

YARMOUTH MACHINE.

From the Black Horfe on Tombland, to the Wreftlers in Yarmouth, fets out twice every day, Saturday excepted, at fix o'clock in the morning, and four in the afternoon, during the fummer, and at nine o'clock each morning, in the winter feafon. Paffengers at 4s. each.

The IPSWICH and NORWICH NEW COACH,
By Way of Thwaite, Eye, Hoxne, Brockdish, Harleston, and Bungay,

Sets out from the Golden Lion Inn, at Ipfwich, every Monday, Wednefday, and Friday morning, at feven o'clock, and from the Bell Inn, Hog-hill, Norwich, every Tuefday, Thurfday, and Saturday morning, at the fame hour. Carries four infide paffengers at 12s. each, and one outfide at 6s. Short diftance at 3d. per mile. Infide paffengers to be allowed 14lb. luggage, and all extra at 1d. per lb.

LONDON STAGE WAGGONS.

From Meffrs. Marfh's on Tombland, to the Bull in Bifhopgate-ftreet; and Meffrs. Jackfon, Dewing and Buck's, from St. Giles's, to the Green Dragon, in Bifhopgate-ftreet, fet out on Tuefday and Friday, and come in on Monday and Thurfday, every Week.

BURY WAGGON,

From the Star, in the Market-place, Norwich, comes in on Mondays and Thurfdays, and fets out on Tuefdays and Fridays in the afternoon.

BARGE.

The barge goes from the Wherry Staith every Monday and Thurfday for Yarmouth, and returns on Tuefday and Friday.

I

---

several well-known local gentlemen. The inn seems to have retained its gastronomic reputation, since it was a favourite haunt of the diarist Parson Woodforde a century later. He usually patronised it on his frequent visits from Weston Longville and was more likely to dine there than at the Angel before going to the play or seeing relatives off on the night coach to London.

Most of the market inns provided for long-distance coaching traffic; by the second half of the eighteenth century stage-coaches left one or other of the inns along the Walk almost daily with mail and passengers for London and there were equally frequent services to all parts of East Anglia.

For shorter journeys it was possible to hire a post-chaise from the King's Head and hackney carriages plied their trade in the city itself. The traffic congestion can only be imagined. There seems to have been little attempt by the coach operators to avoid market-days and all vehicles and their lively teams had to be manoeuvred out through the narrow gateways of the inns, between the divers obstacles in the Market itself and into the jammed lanes leading out of the city. Indeed, within towns as well as on the open road, coach travel was hazardous in the extreme. Collisions were only too frequent, especially

The coaching timetable from William Chase's 1783 Norwich Directory.
(Local Studies Library)

when differences of opinion arose about right of way, since there was as yet no obligation to keep to the left. Pedestrians were at risk from flying hooves and were forced to flatten themselves against house-walls to avoid being trampled. As for the passengers, few embarked on their journeys without deep trepidation and lavish fortification with alcohol. It is no wonder that Parson Woodforde's sister Jane was shaking 'like an aspin leave' as she set off at midnight from the Angel on the first stage-coach journey of her life. He offered fervent prayers for her safety.

The volume of coach and carriage traffic in the market-place showed no signs of diminishing in the early days of the nineteenth century. Even the coming of the railway in 1842 relieved the pressure only gradually. Passengers were wary of this revolutionary form of transport and carriers found it more convenient to pick up goods from the inns.

FOR the market-place, as for the rest of the city, the nineteenth century was an age of improvement – albeit improvement at a somewhat leisurely pace. Even in the 1780s severe inconveniences in the city centre were becoming a matter for public comment. The editor of the first Norwich Directory, William Chase, was especially critical and his introduction to the Directory included a list of measures for amelioration – or, as he put it, 'polite advancement'. Passage through the city, he wrote, was 'difficult, dark, and dangerous'. It would be made much easier if the access lanes into the market-place from Rampant Horse Street were to be widened and Back of the Inns opened up to carriages, or, better still, if a road were constructed linking the Bell Inn with King Street across the Castle Ditches. Moreover, the city was 'horribly paved' and, at the very least, Gentlemen's Walk should be properly flagged and protected from the carriage-way with posts; and, excellent though the Saturday Market was, it would be greatly more convenient if goods on sale could be classed and ranged methodically into rows or lanes crossing each other at right angles. But the chief target

Early nineteenth-century print of the vegetable market. From a lithograph by L. Hague after the drawing by David Hodgson.
(Norfolk Museums Service)

for Chase's strictures, and perhaps the motivation for his Directory, was the absence of street naming and house numbering, a most serious disadvantage in a city 'abounding in opulence and fashion'. Chase took it upon himself to devise a scheme of numbering, beginning with the market-place itself and proceeding systematically with the streets leading off it.

Most of Chase's ideas were prophetic rather than immediately practicable. It was one thing to devise a numbering system, quite another to persuade shopkeepers to dispense with their swinging shop-signs, and householders to paint numbers on their doors; and so far as public works in general were concerned, the city's textile-dominated economy had been badly affected by the loss of overseas markets due to the French wars. It was no time to talk about civic improvement, however desirable. By 1801, when Peck published a new edition of the Directory, little had been accomplished beyond the paving of the Walk with Scotch granite sets, although the editor commented favourably on the 'superior appearance' which shops on the market-place had assumed.

These limited changes were more cosmetic than fundamental. In the early nineteenth century the city centre was still squalid and dirty, ill-paved and badly lit. The provision Market had been re-surfaced at least twice during the eighteenth century, but only with seashore-flint pebbles, which harboured rotting

filth and were easily dislodged. The seemingly endless problem of clearing away horse manure was no nearer solution; while traffic congestion in and out of the Market was as bad as ever. By now public authorities everywhere were becoming pressingly aware of the need for better urban hygiene and from 1805 a series of Improvement Commissions were set up in Norwich to tackle the problems of paving, lighting and cleansing the streets. But progress was slow. Until 1825 the Council had no powers to levy a regular local rate and the financing of public works depended on the city's rents and tolls, private subscription, and long-term borrowing, leading to a heavy municipal debt. It was not until 1863 that money could be found to pave the Walk with good 3-inch York flags, complete with kerbstones; and only in 1874 were Brigg Street and the market-place re-covered with wood blocks – easier on the feet, but hardly less unhygienic than the former cobbles.

But one remarkable innovation reached the market-place early in the century through the enterprise of the privately owned Norwich Gas Company. In 1820 the first iron gas pipes were laid and soon 'The Gasolier' stood in solitary magnificence in a central position. It was the first gas-lamp in the city and for contemporaries it must have shone with incredible brightness in comparison with the oil-lamps it replaced, despite the limited spread of its beams. It remained in place for sixty years until supplanted in its turn by two electric lights, deemed to be cheaper and cleaner.

At long last, by mid-century, most of the main streets had been given name-plates, and a programme was in force to modify the ancient street system.

The four-branched 'Gasolier' photographed in 1854. It is seen standing in front of the entrance to Davey Place, which was cut through between the Walk and Back of the Inns in 1813.
(Local Studies Library)

View of the Market looking north. About 1850. The 'Gasolier' can be seen in the centre of the picture and the Royal Hotel, built on the site of the Angel in 1845, is in the right foreground.
(Norfolk Museums Service)

Davey Place had been cut through as early as 1813, to make a more direct connection between the Walk and Back of the Inns. Exchange Street was completed in 1828 and (as part of a continuing improvement scheme) London Street was widened in 1856.

Much new building took place in the city centre during the second half of the century: several houses round the Market were given new facades – with the loss, unfortunately of some charming eighteenth-century shop-fronts; the Guildhall underwent a face-lift and acquired some Victorian embellishments, including an anachronistic clock-turret; and the old Angel Inn was reorganized, to re-emerge as the Royal Hotel, – named to honour Queen Victoria.

Most radical of all, the malodorous and dilapidated Fish Market, that had stood near the Guildhall for more than seven centuries, was swept away, to be replaced by a grandiose edifice in neo-classical style designed by the County Surveyor, Mr E. Benest. The project was beset with difficulties. There was public outrage when a workman was killed by falling masonry on the site; the unfortunate Mr Benest, accused, rightly or wrongly, of accepting bribes from contractors, was forced to resign; and the Corporation was

The Guildhall today with its Victorian embellishments.

A photograph of the old Fish Market taken from Guildhall Hill, looking towards St Peter Mancroft, 1856.
(Local Studies Library)

The new Fish Market – in the middle distance, with the Lumber Market in the foreground. The Guildhall is in the background on the left.
(Local Studies Library)

The closing of the Fish Market, January, 1914.
(Local Studies Library)

obliged to take over when the builders failed to complete. When, finally, this curious building was opened in 1860, it was to have only a short life, falling victim in 1914 to the need for more office space.

Although the wholesale fish trade was transferred to much more salubrious premises in Mountergate Street, the memory of the 'old' Fish Market lingered on. As late as 1963, a letter to the Eastern Evening News recalled the raucous voice of a Mr Callaghan, whose cries of 'Fish' carried as far as the cab-rank on the Walk. According to the writer they went thus:

> Ki-hipper buyers, ber-louter buyers, hup the Laen [Lane] you go together. Crab buyers, crab buyers, all the stalls. Fish buyers, fish buyers, hup the Laen you go together. Mack'rell buyers, pinks and browns, 'Arridge pink at 2 bob, Southwool brown at 'alf a dollar. Fish buyers, hup the Laen you go together.

By 1914 a ponderous range of miscellaneous offices and hotels stretched between St Peter Mancroft and the Guildhall, replacing nearly all the 'dwellings' of the eighteenth century. The rump of Mr Benest's grand Fish Market was incongruously embodied into the rear of the municipal buildings next to the Guildhall.

Traffic flow through the market-place had gradually become less disorganized in the course of the nineteenth century. The 1825 legislation encouraging, if not actually compelling, drivers to keep

to the left must somewhat have eased the chaos; and a roadway alongside the Walk linking Brigg Street with the new Exchange Street made it easier for wheeled vehicles to keep a defined north/south route. The number of coaches and carriers leaving the inns began to diminish (albeit slowly) after the coming of the railway in 1842, and hackney cabs were, in due course, neatly arranged in a rank along the Walk by order of the Norwich Board of Health.

One late-Victorian amenity, however, was opposed on all sides. Between 1878 and the end of the century, one tramway company after another put forward their schemes, only to be met with solid refusals on the grounds of the nuisance and discomfort which would be caused by the installation and working of these monsters. But eventually resistance crumbled. By 1900, 16 miles of track had been laid in the city and trams plied along the Walk.

William Chase's dream of neatly aligned and classified stalls on the provision market had not been realized, as the photograph of trams shows; nor was it likely to be as long as so many of the stalls were privately and variously owned. But after the 1914–18 War the first measures towards uniformity were taken when the Markets Committee gradually bought up all the stalls with the laudable aim of encouraging ex-service men to hire them in order to make a living on the Market. When eventually, the ownership of all of them was vested in the Council, the Committee took over the responsibility for their upkeep, for the supply of electricity, and for the provision of protective canvas tilts.

This was a first small step towards the dramatic reorganization of the whole market area that was carried through in the 1930s. It had been obvious for a long time that only revolutionary change could update the higgledy-piggledy market-place and the motley assembly of outgrown civic buildings sufficiently to meet the needs of twentieth-century commerce and modern local government. By the 1920s the duties and responsibilities of city administration had once again outstripped all available space. The miniscule Guildhall had become no more than a token civic headquarters and the many new departments called for to implement higher standards of public health and welfare were squeezed anyhow into all corners of the municipal offices.

Saturday morning in the Flower Market, 1914. In the background, office buildings, the Guildhall and Chamberlain's store.
(Local Studies Library)

The rear of the municipal buildings incorporating the north wing of the Fish Market. Photographed just before their demolition in 1938.
(Local Studies Library)

Trams along the Walk, 1929.
(Local Studies Library)

NORWICH MARKET PLACE IN 1950.

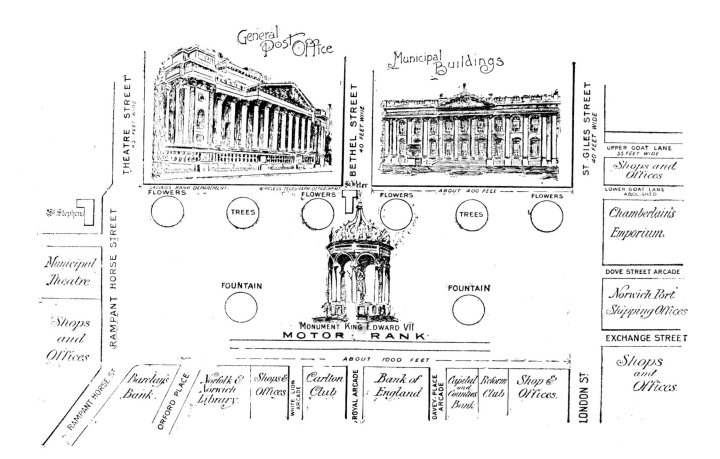

Many people had plans for the Market. This grand metropolitan fantasy, put forward in all seriousness by Mr W. J. Botterill in 1907, got no further than the sketch pad, which is fortunate, as the city would have lost its medieval Guildhall.
(Local Studies Library)

The eventual solution was a bold and far-reaching one. There were to be no half measures, despite the economic stringencies of the 1930s. The scheme involved the complete demolition of the range of miscellaneous municipal buildings and offices that straddled the market-place between St Peter Mancroft and the Guildhall, as well as some nondescript houses bordering Market Street – none of them, fortunately, of especial architectural or historical interest. In their stead, standing high above the newly opened up market-place and spanning its entire breadth, arose the fine new City Hall – the joint work of two architects, C. H. James and S. Rowland Pierce. Not everyone liked it, of course. It was criticized for being too austere, too influenced by an acknowledged dependence on Scandinavian ideas; it was variously likened to a railway station and a public convenience; and there were strong feelings about the expenditure of so many millions of borrowed money at a time of depression and unemployment in the city's boot and shoe industry. But now, when 50 years have passed,

The corrugated iron police station, with the new City Hall rising behind it.
(Local Studies Library)

few would quarrel with the concept, and if doubts linger about the building they are rarely voiced. Many will agree with Nicholas Pevsner, who believed that Norwich City Hall will 'go down in history as the foremost English public building between the Wars'.

In parallel with its building went a complete refurbishment of the provision Market. The untidy hotchpotch of booths, tents, and stalls was swept away, to be replaced by the methodically arranged rows that William Chase had hoped for in 1783.

Demolition 1. The municipal buildings come down in 1938. The low building on the left is the police station. The new City Hall can just be seen in the background on the right with, in front of it, a glimpse of the north wing of Mr Benest's Fish Market.
(Local Studies Library)

Demolition 2. Also in 1938, the old market stalls are flattened. The photograph is taken from near the Sir Garnet Wolsey public house.
(Local Studies Library)

When they had been provided with their familiar, multi-coloured tilts a townscape was created that has become as much a symbol of Norwich as the silhouette of the Cathedral.

Superficially, the Market today appears little changed since the dramatic transformation of the 1930s. However, over the last decade or so improvements have been carried out in the interests of hygiene and efficiency that would have astonished our forbears – whose only amenity was the well near the Guildhall. Many of the 205 stalls are now lock-up units; traders handling food have been provided with refrigeration and with the hot and cold water and washing facilities called for by legislation; and, although the preservation of the open-air market

allied to the rapid spread of car ownership, have produced fundamental alterations in shopping habits. One consequence has been the burgeoning of out-of-town supermarkets run by national chains where, because of centralized buying policies, food-stuffs, and in particular fruit and vegetables, can be sold pre-packaged and of a uniform quality. The threat of competitive pressure on city-centre traders is obvious. But if this presents a danger to the Market it is not evident. Although fruit and vegetable stalls are less numerous than they were, they are still plentiful and well patronized, providing, collectively, a range of choice that no supermarket can match. Nowadays, however, few stallholders bring their own market-garden crops direct to market. Locally grown produce

The concept: a drawing by the architects of the new City Hall and the reconstruction of the market-place.
(Local Studies Library)

atmosphere remains the declared aim of the Markets Committee, some concessions have been made to customer-comfort by the provision of gangway coverings.

There are other more insidious and less perceptible trends which may in the long run bring changes to the trade and life of the Market. Since the last war, and particularly over the last decade, revolutionary developments in the mechanisms of wholesale distribution,

is sold side-by-side with exotic merchandise from the EEC countries and the Middle East, both delivered to the Market by wholesalers' lorries. Some local commodities have become specialist items, sought after by those who look for the disappearing flavours of native varieties.

What then of the long-term future of the centuries-old provision Market, whose mainstay of trade has always been the distribution of the produce of the region and the supply of food to the population of the city and its environs? It may be that the way lies, as the Markets Committee sees it, in the diversification of the goods and services available on the Market, with the consequent encouragement of a new type of small trader. Already health-food and fast-food stalls cater for the gastronomic tastes of the 1980s, watch-repair shops and heel-and-toe bars offer an on-the-spot service, while cosmetics, videos, and paper-backs are the modern equivalent of the hats, pattens, and ballad-sheets of the eighteenth century. But whatever the future holds, the Market's long-proven resilience will surely allow it to evolve a viable role, while never losing its traditional ambience.

Queen Elizabeth – now the Queen Mother – at the opening
of the City Hall, October 29th, 1938, with the Lord
Mayor, Mr C. Watling.
(Local Studies Library)

Short Bibliography

Addison, William, *English Fairs and Markets* (1973).

Barringer, J.C., ed., *Norwich in the nineteenth century* (1984).

Bayne, A.D., *A Brief History of Norwich and its Manufactures* (1864).

Blomefield, Francis, *An Essay towards a Topographical History of Norfolk* (1806 edition) III.

Corfield, Penelope, 'A provincial capital in the late seventeenth century: The case of Norwich', in Peter Clark and Paul Slack, eds., *Crisis and Order in English Towns, 1500–1700* (1972).

Davis, D., *A History of Shopping* (1966).

Dunn, Ian and Helen Sutermeister, *The Norwich Guildhall* (City of Norwich in conjunction with Norwich Survey).

Green, B. and Young, R.M.R., *Norwich: the growth of a city* (1981 edition).

Hudson, W. and J.C. Tingey, *The Records of the City of Norwich* (1906–10).

Kirkpatrick, J., *Streets and Lanes of the City of Norwich* ed. W. Hudson (1889).

Mackie, Charles, *Annals of Norfolk, 1801–1850* (1901 edition).

Muskett, Charles, *Costumes, processions and pageantry* (Corporation of Norwich, 1850).

Rye, Walter, *Depositions taken before the Mayor and Aldermen 1549–1567 and Extracts from the Court Books, 1666–1688* (1905).

Woodforde, James, *The Diary of a Country Parson, 1758–1781* ed. John Beresford (1926).

Norwich Trade Directories: Local Studies Library.

Handbooks and Reports of the Markets Committee: Local Studies Library.

Principal Manuscript Sources in the Norfolk Record Office

Norwich City Court Rolls, 1285–1341.

Norwich Private Deeds: St Peter Mancroft, 1240–1377.

Norwich Cathedral Priory Private Deeds: St Peter Mancroft.

Norwich City Assembly Books.

Norwich Mayor's Court Books.

Minutes of the Markets Committee, 1721–1728.